JUNIOR SURVIVAL LIBRARY

Masters of Land and Water

THE FROG
AND
THE TOAD

Mike Linley

ANGLIA
Television Limited

Boxtree

Key to abbreviations

lb	pound
gm	gramme
kg	kilogram
in	inch
ft	feet
yd	yard
cm	centimetre
m	metre
km	kilometre
sq mile	square mile
sq km	square kilometre
kph	kilometres per hour
mph	miles per hour

First published in 1990 by Boxtree Limited
Copyright © 1990 Survival Anglia Limited
Text copyright © 1990 Mike Linley

Front jacket photograph:
Survival Anglia/Mike Linley
(Poison Dart Frog, Costa Rica)
Back jacket photograph:
Survival Anglia/Mike Linley
(Golden Toad, Costa Rica)

Line drawings by Raymond Turvey

British Library Cataloguing in Publication Data
Linley, Mike
    The frog and the toad.
    1. Frogs & toads.
    I. Title   II. Series
    597.8

ISBN 1-85283-070-0

Edited by Miranda Smith
Designed by Groom & Pickerill
Typeset by Rowland Phototypesetting Limited
Bury St Edmunds, Suffolk

Printed and bound in Italy
by OFSA s.p.a.

for Boxtree Limited,
36 Tavistock Street,
London WC2E 7PB

Contents

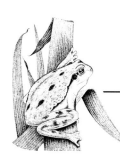

Frogs, toads and their relations 4

The amphibian body 6

Frogs and toads worldwide 8

Moving about 10

Sleeping habits 12

Courtship and mating 14

The egg 16

The tadpole 18

Parental care 20

Finding food 22

Defence against predators 24

Camouflage 26

Frogs, toads and man 28

Glossary 30

Index 31

Acknowledgements
    and Notes on author 32

Frogs, toads and their relations

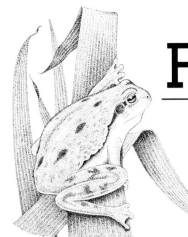

Frogs and toads belong to a group of animals called **amphibians** that includes newts, salamanders and the very strange worm-like caecilians. Salamanders and newts are very similar to frogs and toads in their habits, diet and reproduction. They have a long body, four limbs and a tail. Caecilians look, and live, just like giant earthworms in moist soil, usually in the warm tropics, where they feed on worms and other soft-bodied insects. Some caecilians may reach 60 cm (2 ft) in length.

The word amphibian comes from two Greek words, *amphi-* meaning 'dual' and *bios* meaning 'lives'. An amphibian normally begins life as an **aquatic** tadpole that breathes with **gills** underwater. Then it changes to an air-breathing adult that has lungs and lives on land. This change from one life to the other is called **metamorphosis**. There are exceptions

Toads are usually warty and dry to the touch.

Frogs have damp skin and long hind legs.

to this. Some amphibians do not have tadpoles and never go near water, while others never come out onto land and remain aquatic all their lives.

Frogs and toads are known as **anurans** and are the most successful of all amphibians. The main feature that sets anurans apart from all other amphibians is that they are tailless in the adult stage. The anuran body is much shorter. The hind pair of legs are larger and more powerful than the front pair, and they have **evolved** to be especially good for hopping and leaping.

Most frogs and toads are **nocturnal** and have large eyes that bulge out of the tops of their heads. Frogs and toads are often very hard to tell apart. Frogs normally have a smooth, moist skin, very long hind legs and are never found far from water. Toads tend to have a rough, dry, warty skin, short hind legs for walking rather than leaping, and can be found living in very dry conditions. There is no real scientific distinction between them.

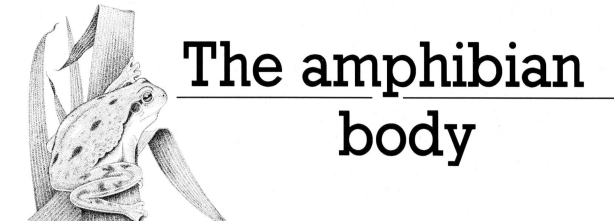

The amphibian body

Amphibians are **cold-blooded**. They do not produce body heat, and this means that their body temperature is always the same as the air around them. It is also why they always feel cold and clammy to the touch.

Amphibians breathe by taking in air through the nostrils into the lungs. The skin on their chins moves up and down all the time,

pumping the air in and out. They are also able to take air directly into the blood system through their moist skin.

One of the biggest problems facing frogs and toads is how they can keep enough water inside their bodies. Because they have such thin skin, water **evaporates** from their bodies very quickly – especially during hot, dry weather. Many anurans avoid water loss by being active only at night when it is cooler, and never venturing far from water. Frogs and toads do not drink. Instead, they **absorb** water through the skin while sitting in a pond or hopping about in the rain.

Some desert-living species, like the Holy Cross Toad, store water inside the body and remain hidden underground for long periods. Aborigines in Australia have learnt to locate

The Tailed Frog

Although frogs and toads do not have tails, there is one species living in North America that, at first sight, appears to have one.

The Tailed Frog lives in cold, fast-flowing streams. What appears to be a tail is in fact a small tube that is used to pass **sperm** into the female's body during the breeding season. Most frogs spray the sperm over the eggs once the female has laid them, but in this case, the currents in the streams are so strong that this would be impossible.

Frogs and toads have rounded bodies with four limbs.

6

their burrows, dig them out and gently squeeze the toad in the palm of the hand to obtain a thirst-quenching drink of pure water.

A frog's head is usually broad and flat, and the mouth very wide. Frogs and toads do not have true teeth, but some have **serrated** jaws and others bony projections. Some of the larger species, such as the African Bullfrog,

have a painful bite. In fact, if prodded with a broom handle, they seize it in a vice-like grip, leaving large marks in the wood.

Anurans usually have four toes on each of their front feet and five on each of their back legs, the toes being joined by a web of skin. In some species, the toes end in suckers which enable the amphibians to climb branches and cling to leaves. In some aquatic species, the toes of the hind feet end in sharp claws which are used for tearing up prey.

Salamanders have long bodies and tails.

Frogs and toads worldwide

Shallow pools make an excellent habitat for frogs and toads.

Some frogs and toads are entirely aquatic.

There are around 3,500 known types of frogs and toads throughout the world. They are found on every continent apart from Antarctica. Anurans also live in nearly every type of **habitat**, from open grassy plains to high mountains, and from deserts to tropical rainforests. In the Americas, anurans are found from the tip of Tierra del Fuego in the south, to within the Arctic Circle in the north. Frogs and toads are found all over the African continent apart from the hottest parts of the Sahara desert, across the whole of Europe with the exception of Siberia, and into Australasia. They have even found their way to places as remote as New Zealand and the Seychelles.

Some species of anuran have an enormous range. The European Common Frog (*Rana temporaria*) is found throughout Europe and much of Asia, as well as within the Arctic Circle in Scandinavia. Others, like the Golden Toad (*Bufo periglenes*) live in only one spot in Costa Rica and nowhere else on earth.

There are frogs and toads that are completely aquatic such as the African Clawed Frog and the Surinam Toad of South America. Although they spend their entire lives in water, they swim to the surface now and again for a gulp of air. One strange-looking frog that lives in the cold depths of Lake Titicaca, in South America, can breathe underwater through the folds of skin on its body. Its skin is so creased it looks like a giant, wrinkled prune.

Some frogs never enter water. Several species that lay eggs on land go through the tadpole stage inside the egg until a tiny, perfect

The Golden Toad is only found on one hillside in Costa Rica.

frog hatches out. Even in some of the world's hottest, driest deserts, frogs and toads can be quite plentiful. In Arizona in the USA, Spadefoot Toads may lie buried for many months, even years, under the parched sand, just waiting for the seasonal rains to fall. When they do, it is a race against time for the toads which have to feed, find a mate and **spawn** in the temporary pools, before digging down into the sand for another year or so.

No frogs or toads can actually live in seawater, but the Crab-eating Frog of south-east Asia is found around salty mangrove swamps. There it feeds, as its name suggests, mainly on fiddler crabs. One of the world's largest toads, the Marine Toad of south and central America, is often found in coastal areas or on small islands where the only available water for breeding is slightly salty.

Record-breakers

Anurans vary enormously in size. The world's smallest is probably the Gold Frog of Brazil that reaches a length of around 1 cm (less than ½ in) when fully grown. The world's largest frog is the Goliath Frog of west Africa, which can reach a body length of 35 cms (13½ ins) and a weight of over 3 kgs (6½ lbs). The world's largest toad is Blomberg's Toad from South America, which is as big as a dinner plate.

Moving about

Anuran tadpoles have long, muscular tails with a fin above and below. Side to side movements of the tail push the tadpole forwards through the water and this is their only means of movement. When frogs and toads metamorphose into adults, they lose their tails, so they have to rely on their new limbs for getting around.

Most toads have large, round bodies and short hind legs, and crawl over the ground using all four legs. They may also be able to hop over short distances. Frogs normally have long, muscular hind legs and can leap many times their own body lengths.

When a frog is about to jump, it raises the front part of its body high off the ground, then it springs into the air. Landing is a bit of a hit or miss affair because, as it jumps, the frog closes its eyes in order to protect them. The front legs and chest usually hit the ground first. Some frogs make just one leap at a time, while others perform several very quickly and cover a great distance.

Frogs that spend most or all of their time in water have large webbed hind feet. An aquatic

The Malaysian Gliding Frog uses its webs as tiny parachutes.

Tree Frogs have strong suckers on their fingers and toes.

frog will hold its arms close to the body. As it brings its hind feet forward, the toes are held close together. When it kicks, the toes spread apart and the webbing between them stretches to act as a large flipper.

Some frogs live in trees and have no webbing between the toes, but have a large, disc-shaped sucker at the end of each toe and finger. The underside of the sucker is covered in rough skin that enables the frog to climb up uneven surfaces like the bark of a tree. On smooth surfaces such as leaves the frog uses sticky **mucous** on its toes and underside to cling on. Some tree-frogs have enormous webs on their front and back feet. These are not for swimming. Instead they act as four little parachutes to slow down the amphibian's fall as it leaps from a tree-top – the nearest thing there is to a flying frog.

Leaping contests

In North America, frog-leaping contests are very popular. The contestants are bullfrogs, America's largest frog, and the contest is the furthest distance travelled over three leaps – usually with someone jumping up and down behind! The record stands at 6.55 m (21 ft 5¾ in). This is about 64 times the frog's own body length.

Sleeping habits

Not all frogs and toads live in a climate that is ideal for them all the time. In **temperate** regions, the winters are so cold that amphibians have to **hibernate**, while in deserts the summers are so hot and dry that the frogs and toads need to **aestivate**.

In northern Europe, the Common Frog hibernates from late November to the end of

The African Bullfrog sleeps through the dry season in a watertight sac.

February, depending on the weather. As the days and nights get colder, the frogs become less and less active, movement becomes difficult and they stop feeding altogether. In order to escape being eaten by **predators**, the frogs hide away under logs or large stones. They sleep through the winter months, living on the reserves of fat stored inside their bodies.

Some frogs may hibernate among leaves or other vegetation at the bottom of the pond. Because they are so inactive they do not need

The Australian Bullfrog stores water during the dry season.

much oxygen. They get what they do need by absorbing it through the skin from the water, rather than by using too much energy breathing. The warmer spring weather makes the frogs active again and it is at this time of year that the frogs mate and spawn. Frogs have been found apparently frozen solid in ice, but when the ice melted, the frogs woke up and within a few minutes were hopping around.

Desert-living species have quite the opposite problem. They have to avoid **dehydrating** in the baking hot summer or dry season. In North America, the Spadefoot Toad may spend ten months or more buried up to a metre (3 ft) underground in the dry earth, waiting for the rains to come. When the rain does fall, it is not the water seeping down into the ground that wakes up the toads – that would take too long. It is the vibration of the rain falling that is the trigger that makes the toad dig its way back to the surface.

The African Bullfrog spends the dry season not only buried underground, but encased in a watertight bag that it **secretes** from its skin. When the rains fall again, the frog wakes up in the moist soil, eats its protective bag and then digs its way to the surface.

In Brazil, there is a tree frog that can survive very hot days by wiping a waxy substance, made in special **glands** in its skin, all over its body and legs. The wax hardens and forms a watertight skin so the frog does not lose precious water. When it rains, the frog wakes up and recycles its special skin by eating it.

Sun-bathing

In east Africa, while most frogs are well hidden during the dry season, one species, the Foam-net Tree Frog, is quite happy to sit out in the open sun. Its skin is very watertight and it can expose itself to the baking heat without drying out. Its skin also changes colour from grey-brown to off-white to reflect some of the sun's heat.

Courtship and mating

Frogs and toads that either hibernate or aestivate normally mate and spawn as soon as they wake up in spring or the wet season. In the **tropics** breeding is often linked to rainfall, while in some species, such as some aquatic frogs that live in a more or less constant environment, breeding can take place at any time of year.

Most male frogs and toads (and occasionally some females) are able to croak. The sort of noise they make and how loud it is varies from species to species. The purpose of the croak is to attract a female of the same species in order to mate. To make his call louder, and so carry far greater distances and therefore attract more females, the male amphibian usually has a **vocal sac** that acts a bit like an echo chamber.

The vocal sac can either be a large round pouch under the animal's chin or two smaller ones at either side of the mouth. Sometimes there is even one large one under the chin with two smaller ones coming off it.

The variety of frog and toad noises is incredible, but all members of the same species make the same noise. Around some tropical forest pools there may be 20 or even 30 species all calling on the same night, so it is important that the females know exactly where they will find males of their species.

Once a mate has been found, the frogs go into **amplexus**. This is where the male frog holds on to his mate until she is ready to lay her eggs. The male grasps her with his forearms around her waist or higher up behind her front arms. Frogs are notoriously slippery creatures so, in order to keep a tight grip, the male has rough pads on his thumbs or front legs to keep him in place. These may even be sharp spines that dig into the female's body.

Shedding skin

Like their close cousins, the reptiles, frogs and toads have to regularly shed their skin in order to grow as well as to keep their skin clean and moist. The skin normally splits down the back first and the amphibian pulls it forward by cramming it into its mouth and swallowing it.

Left *Male frogs call to attract a mate.*

These White Tree Frogs are about to spawn.

One species, the little Rain Frog of South Africa, is so fat and rounded that it is impossible for the male to get his arms around his mate. In order to stay with her, he secretes a glue from his underside that literally sticks him to her back. Once she spawns, he stays there until she next sheds her skin.

Not all species find a mate by croaking. One species of *Eleutherodactylus* uses its chin to advertise its presence, sending vibrations in the ground over short distances. One species of frog in Borneo flashes its bright blue feet to attract a mate. It lives around waterfalls that are so noisy that the sound of its call would be drowned out.

The male Rain Frog 'glues' himself to the back of a female.

15

The egg

Most frogs and toads lay their eggs in water. A single female lays clumps or strings that may contain several thousand eggs. The eggs are normally quite small – only a few millimetres in diameter – and each one is enclosed in a protective jelly to prevent predators like fish from eating it.

The number of eggs laid by a particular species varies enormously. The little Poison Dart Frogs of South America may only lay one or two eggs at a time. On the other hand, the Marine Toad – one of the world's largest

Left *The male Midwife Toad carries the egg string for several weeks.*

Below *Common Frogs lay several thousand eggs each spring.*

anurans – may lay an egg string containing up to 30,000 eggs!

After spawning, the jelly round each egg soaks up water, so that a tight lump of frog spawn the size of a walnut will grow to about the size of a large grapefruit. In some species, like the European Common Frog, large numbers of adults gather to breed at the same time and the pond may become a mass of frog spawn containing millions of eggs. This means that any predators in the water, faced with so much food, will not be able to eat all the tadpoles when they hatch because there are too many of them. However, the survival rate is still not very high. From one clump of spawn with several thousand eggs, only one or two frogs will probably survive to adulthood.

Other types of frogs and toad have adopted a different method of helping their offspring to survive. Instead of just leaving thousands of eggs in the pond some species lay far fewer eggs but go to great lengths to protect them. The Blacksmith Tree Frog (so named because its call sounds like a hammer hitting an anvil)

Red-eyed Tree Frogs lay their eggs in trees above water.

Tree frogs

Instead of laying eggs in water, some tree frogs lay them on leaves overhanging water. When the tadpoles develop, the egg mass collapses and the tadpoles drop into the water below. While on the leaves, the eggs can be protected in a sticky foam mass that frogs like the Foam-nest Tree Frog whip up with their back legs. Or the eggs are protected by one of the adult frogs actually sitting on them to prevent them from drying out.

does not lay its eggs directly in the pond or river. Instead, it digs its own little pool next to the water's edge just before the rainy season. It lays its eggs there and the tadpoles hatch out in complete safety. When the rains fall, the level of the river rises, engulfs the frog pool and the tadpoles swim away.

There are several species of frog, like *Eleutherodactylus*, that simply lay eggs on land – under leaves or stones. The tadpole stage is completely missed out. After a few weeks a tiny, fully-formed frog emerges.

The tadpole

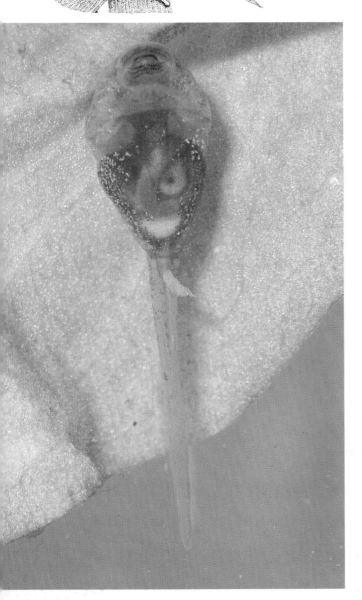

The rates at which the egg develops and the tadpole hatches depends mainly on the temperature of the water. In some species, like the Common Toad, it may take a week or more. In some desert types, where the water temperature can exceed 40°C (104°F), the tadpoles hatch within a day. At first, they cling to the protective jelly with their mouths, and just hang in the water and wriggle occasionally. At this stage they have three pairs of feathery gills that they use to take oxygen out of the water. Within a day or two these disappear inside the tadpole's body and the tadpole, or **larva**, begins to swim around.

Most tadpoles have a small mouth surrounded by rows of little horny 'teeth' that they use to rasp away at vegetation. The majority of tadpoles are vegetarian, but some will rasp away at the bodies of dead animals in the water. Some species have no teeth, only large, gulping mouths that filter out tiny scraps of food floating in the water. Others have enormous teeth and are **carnivorous**, feeding

Tadpoles have a large round body and long flat tail.

Record-breakers

The world's largest tadpole does not belong to the world's largest frog. The Paradoxical Frog of South America has a tadpole that reaches a length of over 20 cms (8 ins) with a body the size of a hen's egg. It may take two or more years for the tadpole to grow to this size. The adult frog, on the other hand, is quite small – only 7 or 8 cm (2–3½ ins) long when fully grown.

Most tadpoles leave the water when the four legs have formed.

mainly on tadpoles of other frogs. One species, the Spadefoot Toad, has tadpoles that eat vegetable matter, but some of them become carnivorous and begin to feed on the others. These tadpoles develop more quickly so, if the pond they are living in dries up in the sun, then at least some of the species will survive.

The tadpole's back legs begin to develop just below the base of the tail. When these are large enough to be recognisable, the front legs begin to form under the skin. When the front legs are big enough, they push their way out but might not appear at the same time. It is usual for a short time to have a three-legged tadpole.

When all four limbs are visible, the tadpole's body begins to alter from a round ball to a more frog-like form. The mouth changes shape and the eyes begin to bulge. Finally, the tail becomes smaller and smaller as it is absorbed into the body, until only a tiny stump remains. At this stage, the tiny frog or toadlet will decide to leave the water, usually at night or during a rain shower. This tiny replica of its parents is less than 1 cm (½ in) long.

Parental care

Some frogs go to extraordinary lengths to look after their tadpoles. The male Midwife Toad even carries the egg string wrapped around his hind legs. He keeps the eggs moist by hopping around during rainfall or taking them down to water. When the tadpoles are ready to hatch,

Live-bearing toad

One tiny type of toad in West Africa, known as *Nectophrynoides*, actually keeps the eggs inside its body where they go through the tadpole stage. The female frog gives birth to four or five tiny toads at a time. This is the only **viviparous** anuran known to science.

he goes down to the water's edge, sits in the water, and the 30 or so tadpoles burst out and swim away.

Some tree frogs like the Marsupial Frog have taken this method one stage further. The female has a large pouch on her back, and the male helps to put her eggs into the pouch using his feet. The tadpoles develop inside, surviving on yolk stored in their stomachs. A few weeks later, fully-formed little frogs emerge from the entrance to the pouch. The Surinam Toad looks after tadpoles in a similar way except that the tadpoles develop in little individual pits all over the back of the female rather than in one pouch.

Perhaps the greatest effort is made by the tiny Poison Dart Frog of Costa Rica. The adult frog rarely reaches 2 cms (1 in) in length. The female lays one or two eggs under a leaf on the forest floor and sits with them until they hatch. Then the tadpoles wriggle onto her back and stay there by using their sucker-shaped mouths. She hops around with them like this for a few days, and then eventually climbs a tree to find a plant called a bromeliad which has a tiny pool of water in the centre of its leaves. She backs into the water and the tadpoles wriggle off. She then climbs back down to the forest floor.

The tadpoles are safe in their tiny pool because there are no predators. However, there is also very little to eat. So the female climbs back up the tree every few days and

Left *Nectophrynoides gives birth to four or five full-formed young.*

20

lays a small number of **infertile** eggs, rich in yolk, for her tadpoles to feed on. When she may have to climb 10 or 15 m (32 or 48 ft) every time, this is a remarkable amount of effort for such a tiny frog.

The male Darwin's Frog also sits with the eggs as they develop, but when they start to wriggle, he bends over and swallows them! They do not go into his stomach but into his vocal sac where the tadpoles grow. After two or three months, the male frog opens his mouth and a tiny frog – one of a dozen or more – can be seen sitting on his tongue.

There is one recently-discovered species of frog in Australia that keeps its tadpoles in its stomach! But it is very rare and very little is known about its life history.

The female Poison Dart Frog carries her tadpoles around on her back.

Finding food

All frogs and toads feed on live, moving **prey**. The vast majority feed on insects and the size of the prey depends on the size of their own mouths and bodies. The European Common Toad feeds on woodlice, spiders, beetles, centipedes, worms and slugs. The Marine or Giant Toad can tackle small snakes, mice and even small rats. The African Bullfrog will eat just about anything that is big enough to swallow including poisonous snakes, giant centipedes, scorpions and even other bullfrogs.

Prey is normally detected by movement. Once seen or felt, the anuran turns in the direction of its prey and lunges. The prey is caught on the end of the frog's sticky tongue, which is attached to the front of the mouth. The insect is not bitten or chewed but simply swallowed – alive. As the frog swallows its prey, its large eyes blink and bulge downwards into its mouth cavity and so help to force the food down its throat.

Some aquatic species such as the Surinam Toad live in very murky water. They have tiny eyes and rely on their sense of touch to find

The African Bullfrog will swallow anything that will fit in its mouth – like a mouse.

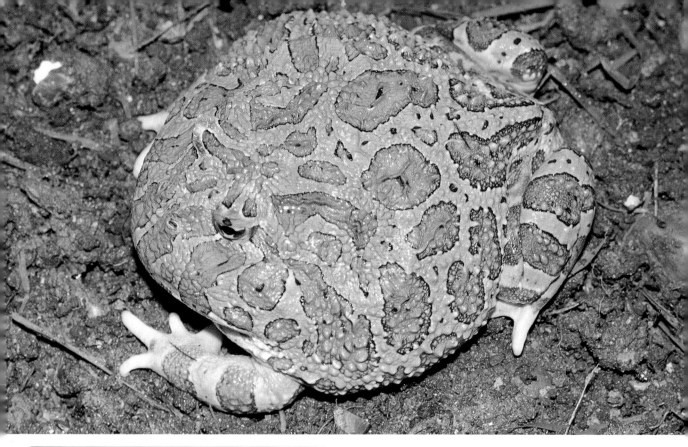

The South American Horned Frog has a mouth as wide as its body.

food. They sit, motionless, on the bottom of the pond or river with their forefeet held out in front of them. The end of each finger is very sensitive and, if touched by a small passing fish or insect, will trigger the toad to lunge forward with its mouth open. It crams the prey in with its feet.

Some species have a highly specialized diet. The Narrow-mouthed Toad, as its name suggests, has a very small mouth, and feeds only on tiny ants and termites. The Mangrove Frog of south-east Asia eats mainly crabs, while the Hairy Frog of west Africa feeds principally on water snails. But in general, frogs and toads are not particularly fussy about what they eat and will take just about anything that is small enough to swallow.

The Argentinian Horned Frog is another matter. It is a **voracious** feeder and is particularly fond of eating other frogs – even the same species. Its mouth extends halfway round its body and it will take frogs up to and including its own size that are far too big to swallow. It simply sits there with half its prey hanging out of its mouth while it digests the other half in its stomach, then it swallows the rest. This is also one of the few frogs that actually attracts its prey. It sits wriggling its fingers or toes, hoping to gain the attention of any passing frogs. As they approach to investigate, the Horned Frog pounces.

Vegetarian frog

Very recently, a frog was discovered in Brazil that had a large number of seeds in its droppings. When observed, the frog was seen to lunge at and swallow the red fruits of the bushes on which it lived. No one knows for certain whether it was looking for and eating the fruits deliberately, or whether it was lunging at tiny insects that were crawling over the fruit. If it was deliberate, this makes it the world's only vegetarian frog.

Defence against predators

Frogs and toads are eaten by a great variety of animals and have developed a wide range of reactions and other adaptations to avoid capture. The most common defence is to leap away when the danger is first sighted or sensed. Failing this, it is always a good idea to swallow as much air as possible to make yourself look as big as you can in the hope that the predator will think you are too big to swallow! Some species become really aggressive and lunge at their attacker with open mouth, even though they have no real teeth. This can be very effective especially with a frog the size of an African Bullfrog which has a mouth big enough to get your fist into. Few predators want to take on that.

Some species rely on colour or markings to avoid capture. Many tree frogs at rest are either uniform brown or green but, when disturbed, they leap away, exposing bright colours along the side of the body and hind legs that are normally hidden from view. This sudden flash of colour is often enough to startle a predator and so allow the frog time to escape. Other species have a pair of large, false eye-markings on their back to make their

The Poison Dart Frog's bright colours warn off predators.

Most poisonous of all

Some of the most powerful poisons occur in the skin of some of the world's smallest and most colourful frogs. The most poisonous frog – and one of the most poisonous of all animals on earth – is the tiny Poison Dart Frog (*Phyllobates terribilis*). The substance in the skin of this bright yellow, 3 cms (1 in) long frog is so powerful that you can feel a tingling sensation in the skin when the frog is handled. Any animal trying to eat one of these frogs will quickly die. If the poison gets into the blood system of a human being just 0.00001 gm (0.000003 ounces) is enough to kill. For thousands of years, South American Indians have caught and roasted these tiny frogs over a fire. They dip their blow darts in the one drop of poison that drips out of each body. It is enough to tip fifty arrows, each one capable of killing a monkey, or a man, in seconds.

Above *Poison Dart Frogs are among the most colourful that exist.*

whole body look like the head of a much larger animal.

Some of the most effective defences against predation involve the use of poisons or other nasty substances that the frogs and toads secrete in their skin. Most toads have glands in the skin that ooze out a white substance if they are attacked. The glands are often found on large warts just behind the toad's head and on its hind legs – the most common places for a predator to strike. The substance varies in strength from species to species. In the Common Toad it is enough to cause a dog to foam at the mouth and vomit. In the Marine Toad, it is powerful enough to kill the dog. Some species can even squirt the poison a metre (3 ft) or more into the face of the attacker.

The warts on the back of the Colorado River Toad ooze out poison.

Camouflage

One of the best ways an animal can protect itself from being eaten by a predator is to avoid being seen altogether. The majority of animals that feed on frogs and toads hunt by sight. They are triggered by the movement of the amphibian, so if the frog sits perfectly still it can often escape. This works particularly well if the frog or toad is **camouflaged**, that is if it is coloured and even shaped to blend in with its surroundings.

Many frogs and toads have mottled patterns on their backs and hind legs to help break up their shape. Those that live in long grass often have stripes down the length of the back. Tree frogs are normally coloured to match their environment – green for the ones that live on the leaves and brown for those that live on the trunk and branches.

The Malaysian Horned Frog lives on the dark forest floor among the leaf litter. Not only is it coloured and patterned to look like a dead leaf, but it also has a short spike on the end of its nose and one ever each eye that look for all the world like leaf stalks. Provided it stays perfectly still it is impossible to see.

Some frogs are coloured on the back for camouflage and yet are really brightly coloured underneath. The Yellow-bellied Toad is a muddy brown colour when viewed from above – perfect for matching the muddy little puddles where it lives. But if a predator comes too close it raises its arms and legs, or even rolls over onto its back, to expose the bright yellow markings underneath. This is a warning to all animals that the toad has a poisonous substance in its skin.

The ultimate camouflage

One of the best forms of camouflage is not only to blend in with the background but to look like something that is totally **inedible**. The little Tree Frog of South America has a body that is coloured black, white and grey, and while it is asleep during the day it looks just like a bird dropping. There are not many animals that are interested in eating bird droppings!

The Green Toad blends in perfectly with its background.

26

Some frogs and toads can partially change colour, although they are not as good as the chameleon. Tree frogs, in particular, are often able to change from bright green to lime green through to greys and browns. This is not always related to their background but can be to do with temperature, time of day or weather.

In some species the male and female are completely different colours and often appear, at first glance, to be two separate species. The rare Golden Toad from the cloud forest of

The Malaysian Horned Frog is coloured and shaped like a dead leaf.

Costa Rica is a good example. The male is a bright golden orange colour and very easy to see on the forest floor, while the female is mottled with red, brown and black, and blends in well with her habitat. This could be because it makes it easier for a female to find a mate. It may also be that it is more important that a male gets eaten rather than a female, who might be carrying thousands of eggs.

Frogs, toads and man

Frogs were once used as weather prophets.

Frogs and toads have been used by people for centuries. Frogs are eaten in many parts of the world. In Europe, the Edible Frogs are a delicacy served up as 'frogs' legs' in French restaurants. However, the Edible Frog is now so rare, that Asian species have to be imported in huge numbers to supply the demand. In North America, the Bullfrog is a particular favourite, as it is a large species with enormous hind legs. The frogs are normally collected at night, after being dazzled by torchlight. On many islands in the Caribbean one large species of frog is known as the Mountain Chicken because its flesh resembles poultry. In Africa, frogs like the Clawed Toad are caught in nets and roasted, and in Brittany, France, the enormous tadpoles of the European Spadefoot Toad are still considered a delicacy.

Man has had other uses for frogs and toads. Tree frogs were once kept in tall jars to predict the weather. If the frog was sitting at the top of the jar, it would be a fine day; if it was at the bottom, it was a sign of rain. For many years the African Clawed Toad was used by clinics for pregnancy testing in women. It is still used in the laboratory and has been introduced into the wild accidentally in many parts of the world, including North America.

Great harm can be done to the balance of wildlife by man's unthinking intereference. The Marine or Giant Toad, is also known as the Cane Toad because it likes to eat the cane beetle, a pest on sugar cane. The toad was deliberately introduced into Australia for this reason but its introduction to that continent has been a complete disaster. Not only has this

The 'Mountain Chicken' is a great delicacy in the Caribbean.

not controlled the beetle (other methods have since been found) but the toad has spread uncontrollably during the last 30 years with a terrifying effect on the local wildlife. The toad has a voracious appetite and eats other amphibians and small mammals as well as snakes. It also has a very potent poison in its skin and any animal trying to eat it or even just investigating it suffers a very painful death. Unfortunately, in this case, it may be too late to prevent the spread of the Cane Toad across the whole of the continent.

Raining frogs

For thousands of years there have been stories of frogs falling from the sky during heavy rainfalls. It may be possible for small frogs to be picked up and hurled about during freak weather conditions, but this does seem extremely doubtful. A more likely explanation is that the heavy rain triggers the emergence of the frogs either from their hiding places beneath the ground or from nearby ponds. The frogs, hopping around in the rain, appear to have fallen from the sky.

Glossary

Absorb To soak up, suck through the skin.

Aestivate To spend a long period asleep or inactive during the summer.

Amphibians Animals that live both on land and in water, for example frogs and newts.

Amplexus The position in which a male frog clasps a female during amting.

Anurans Tail-less amphibians.

Aquatic Living or growing in or on water.

Camouflage The ability to hide from an enemy by appearing to be part of the natural background.

Carnivorous Feeding on the flesh of other animals.

Cold-blooded Having a body temperature that changes with the environment.

Dehydrating Removing water from, losing bodily fluids.

Evaporate To convert or change into a vapour.

Evolved The slow process by which animals change over millions of years.

Gills An organ with very thin skin by which a fish collects oxygen to breathe when it is underwater.

Glands Organs of the body which produces scent and other substances.

Habitat The environment in which an animal usually lives.

Hibernate To spend a long period asleep or inactive during the winter.

Inedible Not suitable to be eaten.

Infertile An egg that has not been reached by a sperm and so will not develop into a tadpole.

Larva The newly hatched stage of a creature that will undergo metamorphosis.

Metamorphosis The change from one stage to another in an animal's life.

Mucous A slimy substance that helps to keep the skin moist.

Nocturnal Active by night.

Predator An animal that hunts and kills other animals for food.

Prey Animals that are hunted and killed by other animals.

Secretes Produces a substance from the glands.

Serrated Having a series of notches.

Spawn The laid and fertilised eggs of amphibians or fish.

Sperm The male seed or reproductive cell.

Temperate The regions of the earth between the tropics and the ice caps with moderate temperatures.

Tropics The warmer regions of the earth near the equator.

Viviparous Giving birth to living young.

Vocal sac The pouch-like part in the frog or toad's throat used when it is croaking.

Voracious Eager to eat great amounts of food.

Index

The entries in **bold** are illustrations.

Aborigines 16
aestivation 10–11, 14
Africa 8, 9, 13, 23
America
   Central 9
   North 6, 8, 9, 13
   South 8, 9, 18, 26
amphibians 4–5, 6–7
   breathing 6
amplexus 14
anurans 5, 6, 7, 8, 10, 22
   ability to climb trees 7
   and water loss 6
   largest 17
   viviparous nature of 20
Arctic Circle 8
Asia 8, 9, 23
Australia 6, 28
Australasia 8

bite 7
Borneo 15
Brazil 23
breeding 14
bromeliads 20

caecilians 4
   food 4
   size 4
camouflage 26–7, **26**, **27**
Caribbean 28
claws 7
cold-bloodedness 6
Costa Rica 8, **9**, 20, 27
courtship 14–15
croaking 14, **14**, 15

defence 12, 24–5
   colour 24
   markings 24
   secretion 25
dehydration 13

egg strips 17
eggs 8, 16–17, **18**, 20, 21, 27
eyes 5

frog-leaping contests 11
frogs 4, 5, 8
   African bullfrog 7, **12**, 13, 22, **22**, 24, 28
   African Clawed 8
   American bullfrog 11
   Argentinian Horned 23
   Australian bullfrog **13**
   Crab-eating 9
   Darwin's 21
   Edible 28
   Eleutherodactylus 15, 17
   European Common 8, 12, **16**, 17
   frozen 13
   Gold 9
   Goliath 9
   Hairy 23
   Malaysian Gliding **10**
   Malaysian Horned 26, **27**
   Mangrove 23
   Mountain Chicken 28, **29**
   Paradoxical 18
   Poison Dart 16, 20, **21**, 24, **24**, **25**
   Rain 15, **15**
   South American Horned **25**
   Tailed 6
   Tree 11, **11**, 13, 17, **17**, 20–1, 24, 26, 27

gills 4

habitat 8, **8**, 26, 27
hibernation 12–13, 14
hopping 5, 10

Lake Titicaca 8
leaping 5, 10
legs 5, **5**, 13

mating 6, 13, 14–15
metamorphosis 4, 10, 18–19
mouths 7, 23

New Zealand 8
newts 4

poisons 24, 25, 26, 29
predators 12, 17, 20, 24, 25, **26**
prey 22
   attracting 23
   crabs 9, 23
   fish 23
   insects 22, 23
   mammals 29
   other anurans 23
   rodents 22
   snakes 22, 29

reproduction 4, 6
Sahara desert 8
salamanders 4, **7**
secretion 13
Seychelles 8
shedding skin 14, 15
Siberia 8
size 9
skin 5, **5**, 13
South Africa 15
spawning 9, 13, **14**, 15, 16–17

tadpoles 4, 5, 8, 10, 17, **18**, 18–19, **19**, 20–1, 28
   feeding 18
tails 6, 10
toads 4, **4** 5
   Blomberg's 9
   Clawed 28–9
   Colorado River **25**
   European Common 22, 24
   Golden 8, **9**, 27
   Green **26**
   Holy Cross 6
   Marine 9, 16, 22, 25, 28–9
   Midwife **16**, 20
   Narrow-mouthed 23
   Spadefoot 9, 13, 19
   Surinam 8, 19, 20, 22–3
   Yellow-bellied 26

vocal sacs 14, 21

warning colours 24, **24**
webbed feet 10–11

Picture Acknowledgements

The publishers would like to thank the
Survival Anglia picture library
and the following photographers for the use
of photographs on the pages listed:

Mike Linley: throughout, except for:
Jen and Des Bartlett 12; Roy Hunt – Doublejay Enterprises 16;
Bruce Davidson 27.

About the author

Mike Linley has had a keen interest in reptiles and amphibians since the age of four, and this is his seventh book on the subject. Mike has a B.Sc. Hons degree in Zoology from Durham University and after teaching for three years he went to Bristol University to research lizard behaviour. He now works for Survival Anglia as a producer of natural history documentaries for the long-running Survival series. He is the author of *The Snake* in the Junior Survival Library.

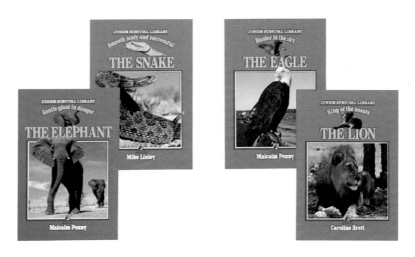

The first four titles in the Junior Survival Library.